14 DAY

The Family Tree Detective

Cracking the
Case of Your
Family's Story

Ann Douglas

illustrated by Stephen MacEachern

Owl

Owl Books are published by Greey de Pencier Books Inc.
179 John Street, Suite 500, Toronto, Ontario M5T 3G5

The Owl colophon is a trademark of Owl Children's Trust Inc. Greey de Pencier Books Inc. is a licensed user of trademarks of Owl Children's Trust Inc.

Distributed in the United States by Firefly Books (U.S.) Inc.
230 Fifth Avenue, Suite 1607, New York, NY 10001

We acknowledge the generous support of the Canada Council for the Arts and the Ontario Arts Council for our publishing program.

About the Author
An award-winning journalist, writer, and teacher, Ann Douglas has published five books and has written extensively on family and parenting for a variety of publications in Canada and the U.S. Ann's first book for children, *Baby Science: How Babies Really Work* (also from Owl Books), is a Book-of-the-Month Club selection and has received great critical and popular acclaim. Ann currently lives in Peterborough, Ontario, with her husband and four children.

Cataloguing in Publication Data
Douglas, Ann, 1963–
The family tree detective: cracking the case of your family's story
Includes index.
ISBN 1-895688-88-4 (bound) ISBN 1-895688-89-2 (pbk.)

1. Genealogy — Juvenile literature. I. MacEachern, Stephen. II. Title.

CS15.5.D68   1999   j929'.1   C98-932286-6

Design & art direction: Word & Image Design Studio
Illustrations: Stephen MacEachern

Printed in Hong Kong

A   B   C   D   E   F

Dedication
To my grandmothers, Mabel Bolton (1900–1995) and Netta Rea (b. 1909), who taught me the true meaning of family.

Contents

Be a Family Detective!

Have you ever wondered what your mother liked to do for fun when she was growing up? Do you ever try to imagine what subjects your grandfather liked—or hated—at school? And what do people mean exactly when they tell you that you're *just like* your mother or your father when they were your age?

Follow Your Nose

Like all good sleuths, family detectives make amazing discoveries. Get on the trail of your family's history and you'll be looking for clues, gathering evidence, and solving mysteries. You'll travel back in time, discovering facts about relatives who lived years before your parents were even born. The more you dig, the more you'll learn.

What's Your IQ?

You don't have to be a genius to be a genealogist. *Genealogy* is the official name for the study of your family's history. It is the story of all the people who are, and who ever were, a part of your family.

Take the time to search a bit and you'll uncover plenty of great tales. You might learn about a time your father broke a window, or that your grandfather's house burned down on the coldest day of the year. Or maybe that your great-aunt was the first girl in the family to finish high school.

Genealogy is a hobby you can enjoy for a long time. It is like a gigantic jigsaw puzzle. Take it out and work at it whenever you feel like it.

This book will tell you everything you need to know to develop your family history detective skills. You'll find out how to get all the information you need, and how to record and organize it. You'll even get exciting tips on how to share your amazing discoveries with others. So, pull out your notebook and get ready to embark on the most fascinating detective case of all: hunting for your family's incredible story.

BRANCHING OUT

Do you want to try something fun? Ask more than one member of the family to tell you about the same event—a birthday party, a family trip, or the time a couple of brothers got into trouble with a bucket of paint. Are their stories identical? Probably not. People's memories are never exactly the same. For instance, your grandmother might have been really mad about something your grandfather said to her on their wedding day—and he might not remember what he said at all! Clever family detectives can learn a lot about people and events from listening carefully to *how* people tell their stories.

From the Roots

So what does learning about your ancestors have to do with you? For one thing, they are—literally!—a part of you. Although there's nobody exactly like you in the world, you share characteristics with your relatives because you share *genes* with them—even if you've never swapped pants.

Swimming in the Gene Pool

Do people tell you that you have your father's smile or your grandmother's artistic ability? What they mean is that you inherited their genes for those traits.

All living things carry genes inside every cell in their bodies. Genes are much too small to see and we don't feel them working, but we know they're there because the chemical messages they send determine how we'll turn out: how tall we'll be, what color eyes we'll have, and whether our hair will be straight or curly, for instance.

BRANCHING OUT

Try your hand at this numbers game. Have you ever wondered how many great-great-great-grandparents you have? List the names of your parents, their parents, their parents' parents, and so on. Then add them all up. Hint: if any of your relatives were married more than one time, you might have enough great-great-great-grandparents to fill a school bus!

Identical twins are the only people who share the same sets of genes—with one another and no one else. In 1979, a set of 39-year-old identical twins met for the very first time. They had been apart since they were five weeks old, but it didn't take the two brothers long to discover that they had a lot in common. They both had dark hair, and were the same height and weight. They drove the same type of car, drank the same brand of beer, and vacationed in the same part of Florida. Their heart rates, brain waves, and intelligence test results were almost identical, and their personalities were so similar that the researchers could hardly tell them apart. How's that for proof of the power of genes?

The Recipe for You

Half of your genes come from your father and the other half from your mother. But that doesn't mean that you are exactly 50% like your father and the other 50% like your mother. Here's where it gets interesting.

Scientists think that *tens of thousands* of genes are needed for the intricate recipe that resulted in you. Because of all the possible ways that all those genes could combine, if your parents tried the recipe again, they would end up with someone entirely different. In fact, your parents could try the recipe millions of times and never get the same person twice. It's like putting coins into a gigantic gumball machine full of different colored gumballs and seeing what you get. Sometimes you get a red, two blues, and a green. Other times, you get a yellow, a blue, and two whites. The possibilities seem endless.

1
Bb   Bb
BB
brown eyes

2
Bb   Bb
Bb
brown eyes

3
Bb   Bb
bB
brown eyes

4
Bb   Bb
bb
blue eyes

Detective Tip

If you have a *dominant* gene for a trait, then the trait it determines will show up. The gene for the trait that doesn't show up is called *recessive*. For example, the gene for brown eyes is dominant and the gene for blue eyes is recessive. That means, if you inherited a gene for brown eyes (B) from one parent and a gene for blue eyes (b) from the other, you would have brown eyes, because the dominant gene cancels out the recessive gene. You could end up with blue eyes, though, even if both your parents had brown eyes, if they both carried the recessive gene for blue and both passed it along to you (see number 4 on the left).

B R A N C H I N G OUT

Here's an excuse to stick out your tongue at the dinner table—and a way to get your parents to stick out theirs, too! Ask everyone around the table if they can roll their tongues like hot dog buns. Can you? Can other members of your family?

The gene that allows you to roll your tongue in a U-shape is a dominant gene. (See the Detective Tip on page 8 for more information about dominant genes.)

Once you've finished the tongue-rolling Olympics, see how many people in your family have ear lobes that are fully attached (a recessive trait) or only half-attached (dominant); freckles (dominant); or dimples (dominant). If you aren't biologically related to your parents (if you're adopted, for instance), you might still have some of these in common. But even if you don't, remember, there's a lot more to a family than just genes. Read on to find out.

It's All Relative

Trying to figure out who's who, and exactly how you're related to the people in your family can make your head spin. Here are some clues to help you keep your family ties straight as you do your research.

Your grandparent's mother and father are your *great-grandmother* and *great-grandfather*.

Your grandmother's or grandfather's brothers and sisters (and their wives and husbands) are your *great-uncles* and *great-aunts*.

Your mother's and father's sisters are your *aunts*. If your aunt is married, her husband is your mother's and father's *brother-in-law*, and your *uncle*.

Your mother's and father's brothers are also called your *uncles*. When your uncle gets married, his wife becomes your mother's and father's *sister-in-law*, and your *aunt*.

Your aunts' and uncles' children are your *first cousins*. If your first cousin is a girl, she is your parent's *niece*. If your first cousin is a boy, he is your parent's *nephew*.

When your first cousins have children, the children will be your *first cousins once removed*. (The word "removed" refers to another generation—either older or younger. In this case, your cousin's children are part of a generation younger than yours.)

If your father and mother are divorced and your mother gets married again to another man, her new husband is your *stepfather*. And if your father remarries, his wife is your *stepmother*.

Your *stepbrothers* and *stepsisters* are the children of your stepmother or stepfather. You might have the same mother or the same father as your stepbrothers and stepsisters.

When you have children of your own, they will be *second cousins* with your first cousins once removed.

BRANCHING OUT

Now you can test your newly acquired knowledge of family relationships by trying this quiz.

1. What would you call your grandfather's sister?
2. If your second cousin had a baby, what would that new baby be to you?
3. What relation are you to your aunt?
4. How do you refer to your father's son from a previous marriage?
5. What do you call your mother's sister's husband?

Answers: 1. great aunt 2. second cousin once removed 3. her niece 4. stepbrother 5. uncle

Growing a Family Tree

Grandparents

Aunts & Uncles

Parents

Cousins

Brothers

Me

Favorite Family Pets

Famous Family Sayings

Many genealogists put their family facts in the form of a diagram, or a *family tree*. It's a great way to make sense of who's connected to whom and where each person fits in. Photocopy this page and fill in details of your own family tree. You can write names and birthdays in the boxes, put tiny photographs in them, or draw pictures of your family members. If you are able to go back farther, or if your family's really big, then take another piece of paper and make a bigger tree and bigger boxes!

Aunts & Uncles

Sisters

Cousins

My Great-Grandparents

Best Family Reunions

Getting Going

Has anyone ever told you that they heard something "straight from the horse's mouth"? When people say that they mean that they got the most accurate information because they got it directly from the source. What better place to start finding out about your family than by going right to the people who know them best—your relatives and family friends.

BRANCHING OUT

Wouldn't it be fun to crack open a time capsule full of things that were popular when your parents were young? You can create your own for future generations to enjoy. Here's what you need to do:

- Find a sturdy, waterproof container with a tight-fitting lid. The larger it is, the more you can fit into it—but the more difficult it will be to store.

- Inside, place items that will give a feel for what it was like to be you in the time you're growing up: an issue of your favorite magazine; photographs of you and the members of your family; hockey cards; a list of your ten favorite movies, books, and games; an autograph book; a postcard from your best friend; or some pawprints from your pet. You might also want to write a letter to yourself that you or your future children can read, spelling out your hopes and dreams for the future.

- Seal the capsule, and label it with the date upon which it is to be reopened (if the box is securely closed, you'll be less tempted to peek at the contents before then). Then store it in a safe place (in the basement, or on the top shelf of your bedroom closet) and forget about it for the next few decades.

There's No Place Like Home

Researching your family history can be a lot like having a TV talk show—with you as the host! You can decide whom to interview and what to ask them. Of course, you'll want to spend lots of time talking to relatives: your parents, aunts, uncles, cousins, grandparents, and so on. But don't forget about the friends of the family who have interesting stories to tell, particularly the people who have known you and your family for a very long time.

Detective Tip

It's the colorful stories about your relatives—both living and dead—that really make your family history come alive. You will probably want to ask the people that you interview to share two types of stories: stories about what you were like when you were little, and stories about their own growing-up years. These tales are great fun to hear because they tell you about the time before you were born or when you were too little to notice what was going on around you—times that otherwise you would know nothing about.

15

Get the Scoop!

Top 3 Secrets to Sensational Interviews

1. Be prepared
The best family detectives are those who plan their interviews ahead of time. Here are some tips:

- Make a list of the people you will talk to by phone, those you will meet with in person, and those you will interview by mail or e-mail.
- Write out a list of questions ahead of time so that you won't forget anything important. (Turn the page for some ideas of what you might ask.)
- Think about what you want to talk about with each person. You might, for example, want your grandmother to tell you stories about what your mother was like as a child, and your uncle to tell you what it was like to be a teenager during the 1970s.

So you want to be a star . . . a star interviewer, that is! When you see a professional journalist interview people on TV, you know that there's an art to getting people to open up to you and share their stories. What you might not realize is that it's actually a whole lot easier than it looks. Here are some tips to help you track down the best stories.

2. Be flexible

- Don't be afraid to add or subtract questions from your list as you go along. If someone tells you something particularly fascinating, you might want to learn more about that rather than asking the other questions on your list.
- Some people have very busy lives, and it may be hard for them to find the time to help you to conduct your research. If you call and the person sounds busy, ask if there would be a better time to call.
- If you're writing to someone, let them know specific things you'd like to find out. Also let them know that you'd be happy to hear about anything else they think is interesting.

3. Have fun

This is the most important secret of all. You're likely to get great answers to your questions if you can make the interviews as fun as possible for yourself and the other person. The name of the game is to enjoy yourself. What you learn along the way is just the icing on the cake!

The Inside Story

Here are some words of wisdom from experienced family detectives:

- Looking for a way to get the conversation started? Ask people you are interviewing to show you old photographs or other family stuff. Having people talk about what is happening in the photos, or explain some of the wonderful things they have collected, may help them remember stories they can share.
- If you're going to call someone out of town, keep in mind they may live in a different time zone. You can find out more about time zones by looking in the front of the phone book. Also, remember that long distance calls are expensive. Be sure to ask your parents if it's okay, and if they can help you figure out the cheapest time to make your call.
- There are plenty of alternatives to the phone, of course. You can send the person an e-mail or a letter by regular mail. Either way, you can attach a photo of your family for fun, or even a copy of something you've drawn.

You can use these pages to help you interview your family members. Photocopy them first so you can have a new form for each person you interview. You'll probably want to record your interview in a notebook or on tape and then fill in the form afterwards.

QUESTIONS ABOUT THE OTHER PERSON

What was your favorite subject in school?

What was the best birthday present you ever received?

What did you do for fun when you were a child?

What was your least favorite thing to do as a child?

What were your favorite musical groups when you were a teenager?

Is anyone in your family a good athlete, a talented artist, or special in another way?

Have you ever used a computer? When was the first time?

QUESTIONS ABOUT ME

How old was I when you first met me?

What was I like?

What games did I like to play?

How well did I get along with other children my age?

How were my birthdays celebrated?

What is the funniest thing I've done in the time you've known me?

Here are some questions you might want to ask when you're conducting your interviews. If you have better questions in mind, terrific! This is your opportunity to ask anything you're curious about.

Now's the time to let your own personality shine through. This space is for you to write in questions that you make up yourself.

My top 3 questions:

1

2

3

Name of person being interviewed

Date of interview

Location of interview

How is this person related to me?

When was (s)he born?

Where was (s)he born?

Does (s)he have any brothers or sisters?
What are their names?

Does (s)he have any children or grandchildren?
What are their names?

Does (s)he have a job? What is it?

What is his/her favorite family memory?

What do I have in common with this person?
(Hint: are you both big hockey fans, or do you
both have dimples, for instance?)

What did I discover in this interview that I
didn't know before?

Things I might want to ask next time

Pulling in the Info

Now that you're thinking about *what* to ask, you'll need to consider *how* you're actually going to do it—and, just as important, how to keep track of all the great stuff you're discovering. (There's no point in digging up all this information if two months later you don't remember who said what!)

Traditional mail and e-mail

Here is a model letter from another family detective (see right) to give you some ideas for writing your own letter to family and friends. If you'd like to get back information, such as where and when the person was born and how many brothers and sisters they have, you can make up a form with specific questions (like the one on page 19) and send it out with the letter.

Chris Jacobs
555 Main Street
Toronto, Ontario
M5M 2M2 Canada
Phone: (416) 555-4555
e-mail: cjacobs@email.com

Dear Uncle Tom:

I haven't seen you since the marshmallow-eating contest at last year's family picnic.

Since then I've become a detective—a family detective, that is. I am writing to you to see if you could fill in some of the pieces for me in our family history. I would be especially interested in hearing from you about what it was like to travel around the world. (Grandma tells me that you travelled after you graduated from university, and that you might have some interesting stories to tell me about your experiences.) I'm also including a form for you to fill in with information that will help me to figure out how everyone fits into the family.

If there are other stories you would like to share about members of our family, I would love to hear them!

You can write back to me at the address at the top of this letter or phone me.

I hope to hear from you soon.

From,
Chris

- Don't forget to include your name, address, phone number, and e-mail address in the letter. Then, people will know how to get in touch with you in whatever way they prefer.
- If you are writing to a relative you haven't met, introduce yourself and explain how you are related (for example, "Your sister-in-law Kathryn is my grandmother").
- Keep copies of the letters you send out. If you're writing your letter on the computer, print out an extra copy and also save a copy on a disk marked "Family History." If you're writing your letter by hand, make a photocopy of the letter before you mail it.
- Keep a check-list for yourself so you'll know whom you've sent letters to—and who has answered you.

Audiotape

Here are some tips on recording your interviews on audiotape:

- Check all your equipment and read over your questions beforehand. Maybe your brother or sister or a friend will do a rehearsal interview with you, which you can play back to find out how it sounds.
- Make sure that the room is quiet. If the radio or TV is on in the background, you'll have a hard time hearing what the person is saying when you listen to the tape.
- At the beginning, state the date, the location, and the name of the person you are interviewing.

- Try to keep the interview as brief as possible. You won't want to listen to hours and hours of tape later on—unless, of course, the person you are listening to is a wonderful storyteller.
- Don't rely on your tape recorder alone. Take notes, too. When you get home, play back the tape and read over your notes to make sure you wrote down the most important parts of the interview.
- Remember to label your tapes with the name of the person you interviewed and the date. You might also write a few words to remind yourself what the person talked about.

Videotape

Here are a few pointers to help you get the best possible results with a video camera:

- It's hard to operate the camera and do the interview at the same time. Why not team up with your cousin or sister or brother. Your partner can operate the camera while you interview half the time, and then you can switch.
- Check your equipment before you leave home. Make sure that the battery is fully charged or that you bring along the adapter that allows you to plug it into a wall outlet instead.
- When you start making your video, introduce yourself and the person you are interviewing—like interviewers do on TV.
- Be prepared with your questions. This will keep things moving along at a good pace so that the tapes will be interesting to play back for others.
- Label your tapes right away to be sure you know what's on each one.

Amazing Family FACT

Families in Mexico pay tribute to their ancestors during an annual celebration known as the Day of the Dead. Between October 27 and November 2 of each year, families invite the spirits of their ancestors to return home to enjoy such delicacies as *gallina en mole* (chicken in a dark, spicy sauce) and *pan de muerto* (a sweet-tasting bread known as "bread of the dead"). Families cover tables with flowers, fruit, vegetables, candles, incense, statues of saints, and photographs of the person being honored. They also visit cemeteries and hire musicians to play the favorite songs of family members who have died.

Staying High and Dry

As you carry out your detective work, you'll want to find a safe, dry place to store your materials. A plastic box with a tight-fitting lid works well. It prevents your audiotapes from getting spilled on while you're having your dinner, and stops your little brother or sister from turning your notes into paper dolls. You might also want to place plastic page protectors in a three-ring binder to hold copies of photographs, letters, or any other special papers you collect along the way.

Here are a few more ideas for keeping everything in order:

• Keep a list of all the people you've interviewed, and whether it was by letter, audiotape, or videotape, so you'll know where to look for information on them.

• Try using file folders or a binder to store your interview notes, photocopied forms, and letters people write to you. Dividers will help to keep things well organized. This may not seem so important in the beginning, but as time goes on and you collect more information, you'll be glad you did.

• Make labels for all your materials right away while what's there is still fresh in your mind. For instance, you might not recognize your great-uncle's voice on an audiotape or be able to read your aunt's signature on a letter, but if you have a good system for storing and labelling you'll be able to find out quickly.

• Keep your computer disks together. Don't forget to print off a hard copy of what's on your disk and save the hard copies in a file in case something happens to the disk.

• Store videotapes and audiotapes in their protective cases so that they're less likely to get damaged.

Would you like to compare notes with other family history detectives? You're in luck! There are plenty of genealogical societies and online discussion groups devoted to the art of digging up family histories. You can find links to some of the best Internet genealogical resources at http://www.familytreemaker.com/links/. Use this as your stepping stone to libraries, archives, genealogical societies, and more. One of the pages within the site, http://www.familytreemaker.com/links/c/c-groups-and-societies.html, contains links to nearly five hundred genealogical societies around the world, including the International Internet Genealogical Society. (That should keep you busy for a while!)

You can also contact these organizations listed below, and they will put you in touch with genealogical societies in your own community:

In Canada:
Genealogy Unit
National Archives of Canada
395 Wellington Street
Ottawa, Ontario K1A 0N3
(613) 996-7458

In the United States:
National Genealogical Society
4527 17th Street North
Arlington, VA 22207-2399
(703) 525-0050 or
(800) 473-0060

Looking for Clues

Believe it or not, some of the best clues to your family's story are under your very own roof. They are the kinds of treasures that every family detective wants to find because they provide lots of information about family members, as well as the times they lived in. Don't forget to get permission before you start snooping!

Hide-and-Seek

While attics, basements, and closets are often used to store old photo albums, letters, and other assorted paraphernalia, people in your family might have their own special places. Who knows? Maybe your grandparents keep the most valuable treasures of all stored in an old shoebox under their bed!

Sometimes people forget about all of the useful goodies they have tucked away. This is where your detective skills really kick in. You can help to jog family members' memories by asking them if they have any of the following items. Each of them can provide you with clues about your family's past. Consider the evidence for yourself.

CLOTHES

Can any family members show you their prom dress, wedding dress, tuxedo, or other special clothes? Don't forget to ask about old everyday clothes, too. Maybe your parents have a T-shirt from their favorite band tucked away somewhere. Not only will you learn about what was in style in days gone by, you'll also find out other interesting tidbits, such as what kind of music someone listened to, or whether a particular relative kept up with every fashion trend.

BIRTH AND DEATH ANNOUNCEMENTS

People often announce the births and deaths of family members in the newspaper. It is an easy way to share this news with others. (It was especially so over a hundred years ago, before people were using telephones.) Look at any birth announcement in today's paper and, along with the new baby's name, you'll discover lots of useful information about the family involved, for example, the names of brothers and sisters, parents, aunts, uncles, and grandparents. Now, see if anyone kept announcements about your own family members!

BABY BOOKS

This is where parents record landmark information, such as when their child first smiled, walked, and talked. Do your father and mother have their own baby books? Take a peek and learn when they got their first teeth, when they took their first steps, and what their first word was. Did your parents create a baby book for you, too? If they did, find out whether you walked before you talked, or whether it was the other way around. When did you take your first steps? What was your first word? Was it the same as your mother's or father's?

Letters and Postcards

Letters and postcards are often filled with funny stories about things that happened in everyday life. You can also learn about the relationship between the person who wrote the letter and the person who received it by paying attention to the words. Did the writer say how much he or she missed the other person, or use a special nickname, for instance? Does this help to explain why someone kept these letters? Even the postmark on the envelope or postcard can provide you with important clues, such as when it was written and where it was mailed.

Catalogues

If you can, try to get your hands on an old catalogue. You can find out what clothes people wore at another time, what games were popular, what sports equipment was like, and much more. You'll probably be amazed at how low prices were when your parents or grandparents were growing up. That doesn't mean that everyone was rich back then. People earned far less money then than they do today, so they had to work just as hard to buy things as we do now. Still, it can be fun to think about how far your allowance would go if chocolate bars still cost only 10 cents apiece!

MAGAZINES AND NEWSPAPERS

Magazines and newspapers not only provide the news of the day, they're also full of photographs that show what people wear, what they eat, what they do for fun, and lots more. Can anybody show you old magazines or papers they've saved? Think about it, there's got to be a reason why someone in your family decided to hang on to this particular newspaper or magazine. See if you can figure out what it is. Is there a photograph of a family member? Is it the source of a favorite family recipe? Maybe there's a story written by or about someone in your family.

REPORT CARDS

Was your father an A-student? Did your mother's love of books start when she was in the first grade? How did they behave in class? You can find out by reading through old report cards. It can be funny to discover how much people change—and how much they stay the same!

AUTOMOBILE BROCHURES

Have you ever wondered what your parents'—or grandparents'—first new car looked like? They might still have the brochure tucked away in a box in the garage. If you're really lucky, you might even track down a photo of them pulling out of the dealership with a big grin on their faces. Do you notice anything different about cars then and cars today? What did they look like? How big were they? Was there such a thing as a seat belt?

TOYS

Are you curious about what your parents played with in the days before video games and home computers were invented? Ask them if they have any old toys tucked away, such as dolls, trucks, teddy bears, and board games.

TICKET STUBS AND PROGRAMS

Someone may be able to show you some old ticket stubs or programs. People tend to hold on to these types of souvenirs when they've had a particularly enjoyable evening out. Ask your relatives if they have programs from plays or concerts they attended or ticket stubs from sporting events or rock concerts. If you're really lucky, they may even sing one of their favorite songs for you!

OLD PHOTO ALBUMS

By looking at old photographs you can discover what your family members looked like when they were younger, what they did for fun, and where they lived. The photos may be labelled with information about who is in the photo, and where and when the photo was taken. If they aren't, try asking other family members if they can fill in any details for you. If you come across something really great, you might want to get a copy made for your own collection of family stuff.

BRANCHING OUT

Find out if anyone in your family has early photographs they can show you. Because very few people actually owned cameras when your great-grandparents were kids, having their picture taken was something very special. Parents and children would spend a long time doing their hair and putting on their finest clothing. And when the photographer asked them to pose for the photo, he meant that they had to stay in exactly the same position—for fifteen minutes! Camera equipment was less sophisticated and much slower than it is today. That meant that even if someone was tired of smiling, had an itchy nose, or had to sneeze, he had to stand perfectly still or else the part of the body that moved would show up as a blurry spot on the photo. So, just be glad the next time someone asks you to "say cheese" for the camera that you have to hold that ear-to-ear grin for only a few seconds at a time.

Globetrotting

If you look into your family's history, you'll probably find out that there have been a number of journeys, big and small, that brought yours to where it is now. Not only is it exciting to hear about these moves, but learning where your family comes from tells a lot about who you are today.

From Near and Far

Sometimes families move short distances—around the corner or across town—other times, around the world. What's fascinating are the stories behind these journeys. Often they are happy tales, such as when people get a new house or move to be reunited with family members. But they also can be sad, for instance when violence and war make it dangerous for people to stay. Any way you look at it, though, a move is always a new beginning.

Amazing Family
F A C T

Families have been on the move for thousands and thousands of years. Anthropologists (scientists who study the origins and development of humans) believe that the first people to arrive in North America walked across a massive land bridge that joined Northeast Asia and North America some 10,000 to 45,000 years ago. This occurred during the Ice Age—a time when parts of North America were covered in sheets of ice that were 3 kilometres (almost 2 miles) thick. When the ice melted, the land bridge was buried under water, and North America's first immigrants—the First Nations peoples—found themselves stranded in the New World, like it or not.

Have Suitcase, Will Travel

Have you ever wondered how your own family ended up living in a certain city or town, or neighborhood? You can find out by doing a little detective work.

Solving the case starts with you. Have you ever lived anywhere other than where you're living now? What about if you go back further into your family's history? For instance, did your parents, grandparents, or great-grandparents move from another country? Find out what made them decide to move, then pull out a map and trace your family's journey from their old home to your present one. What can you learn about the voyage they made? Did they travel by boat, plane, train, bus, or car? How long did the trip take? How did they feel about saying goodbye to the people they left behind? What traditions did they bring with them from their old country? The answers to all these questions will tell you a lot about what makes your family unique.

Detective Tip

Did anybody in your family arrive in North America between the late 1800s and the mid 1900s? They wouldn't have been alone. This was a period of great movement of people, particularly to North America, which was seen as a land of great opportunity. Ellis Island, in New York Harbor, is the site of the largest human migration in modern history. Between 1892 and 1954, 12 million people came through the immigration station at Ellis Island. Today, almost half—over 100 million—of all living Americans have an ancestor who passed through Ellis Island. If you look up Ellis Island, which is now a museum, in the library or on the Internet (see page 39), you can get a taste of both the joy and hardship experienced by those people looking to start a new life in North America.

What's in a Name?

What do you do when you need to get your friend's attention? You just call out his or her name, right?

Did you ever stop to think how often we use people's names? In our daily lives, names identify people and distinguish them from others. You'll discover that names are also important to family detectives because they help them to figure out who's who in a family, and can offer clues to many other things about a person.

First Things First

Consider your own name. It says a lot more about you than you might think. Names often provide hints about *where* people were born. If your family comes from Germany, you might have a name like Helmut or Gretchen. If you were born in France or another French–speaking place, you may be a Pierre or a Celine.

Names can also provide clues about *when* people were born. Just as clothes go in and out of fashion, names also go in and out of style. So, for instance, if you're named Jennifer or Jason—the most popular North American girl's and boy's names in the early 1990s—there's a good chance you were born around that time.

Name Games

Sometimes children are given a "nickname" by friends and family. Often these names stick because they are easier to say than the person's full name, and they are a term of endearment. For example, girls named Elizabeth can be called Liz, Liza, or Beth, and boys named William are often nicknamed Bill, Billy, or Willy.

Sometimes, the nicknames that are the most fun have nothing to do with a person's real name, but describe something about that person's character or appearance. Someone who can run quickly might be nicknamed "Speedy;" someone with long legs might be called "Stretch;" and someone who's always happy might be "Sunny."

Do you have a nickname? Do any members of your family have nicknames? Can you find out the stories behind these names?

Lasting Impressions

Imagine living in a town where four men were all named Tom. You're talking to a friend about Tom, but before you continue, you have to explain which Tom you are talking about. "You know, Tom, the son of Tom," you might say. Or, "Tom, the tailor." After a while, everyone might get so used to referring to Tom as "Tom, the tailor" that they might just call him "Tom Tailor." Presto! He has a last name.

Last names came along to solve problems just like this one. The John who had a father named Peter became known as John Peterson. The Robert who baked bread for a living became known as Robert Baker. And the Sarah who had a house at the top of the hill became known as Sarah Hill. Eventually, these last names—or *surnames*—began to stick with particular families and were passed along regardless of whether they meant anything anymore. That's why it's possible now to find a man named John Cook who burns everything but hot water, a woman named Marjory Short who's six feet tall, a woman named Luanne Big Canoe who doesn't even own a boat, or a man named Mark Rich who has hardly a penny to his name.

It takes keen detective work to keep track of who's related to whom in the history of a family. And it doesn't help that the spellings of surnames changed over time. Why? For one thing, our ancestors weren't great at spelling. Ship captains and government officials not only spelled people's names wrong on official documents, but they often spelled them in different ways on the same piece of paper! Other times, families who came from other countries changed their surnames to make them easier for their new neighbors to spell or pronounce. As a result, "Noblinski" became "Noble," "Savitch" became "Savage," "Blanc" (the French word for "white") became "White," and so on. In some families, siblings ended up with different last names even though they had the same parents. One sibling might choose one spelling of the family name, for example, "Green," and the other sibling might choose "Greene."

BRANCHING OUT

So, what does your name say about you and your ancestors? Start with your first name. Find out from your parents why they chose it. Is it a name that's been passed down in your family, or is it a name that was popular at the time you were born? Maybe your parents named you after a character in a movie or novel they like, or heard the name in a song.

What about your last name? Can you identify any root words in your name and think about what they mean together (for example, Goodfellow = good + fellow). A dictionary may be helpful—some have a list of names and their meanings in a separate section in the front or the back of the book. You can ask your parents to translate the meaning of your name if it's from another country and you don't know the language. You can also ask your parents if they know of any family member who has researched the origins of your family name. If not, ask the librarian at your school or public library to help you to find a book that lists the origins of last names, or go to the family tree maker web site at http://www.familytreemaker.com/ifftop.html and do a search under your family name.

Travelling through Time

W ouldn't it be fun to be able to hop into a time machine, spin the dial, and find yourself back where your grandparents or great-grandparents grew up? That's what researching your family history is about—discovering what life was like in days gone by. We haven't yet invented actual machines to transport us back in time, but there are time machines of another kind, like the ones listed on these pages, that can take you time-travelling in your family's history.

The Local Library

Ask the librarian to help you find books with photographs and drawings of life in a particular place and time. Here are just a few of the discoveries waiting for you on the library shelves: books packed with pictures of old toys, novels set in another time that paint a picture of what life was like then, and books about inventions, such as the telephone and TV, that changed people's lives.

The Video Store

Going into your video store can be like landing in another time as well. Ask someone who works in the store to help you to find fictional (made-up) and non-fictional (true) accounts of life in days gone by. They'll be able to make specific suggestions if you have a certain destination in mind. For instance, you might be interested in movies about the time when the pioneers were settling the land in North America, or what life was like for a child in Europe during the Second World War.

The Internet

This "time machine" runs on search engines. The Internet is a source of tons of great information on what life was like many years ago. Here are a few sites that you'll definitely want to visit:

- The Smithsonian Institution's National Museum of American History (http://www. si.edu/organiza/museums/nmah/notkid/ nmabc.htm). You can discover the origin of the teddy bear, find out what toys Iroquois children played with in the seventeenth century, get a sneak peek at an old schoolroom, and much more.
- The History Channel (http://www.history channel.com/community/ellisisle/newworld. html). You can learn about the challenges that faced the millions of people who emigrated to America, arriving at Ellis Island around the turn of the century, and lots more.
- World Surfari (http://www.supersurf. com/about.htm). Find out what life was like for ancestors who lived in different countries by surfing over to World Surfari. You'll learn about their culture, traditions, and much more, and there's a fun activity to try for each country you visit.

Your Imagination

Close your eyes and imagine what it was like to be living in your grandmother or grandfather's time. Imagine what their house looked like—you can cheat a little if you can find some old photographs—and what they liked to do for fun. Did your grandfather find a secret hiding spot somewhere where he could sit and read his comic books undisturbed? Did your grandmother have a favorite place to meet her friends after school?

Family trees are a great way to keep track of the family, but they can't capture a family's true personality. Here's your chance to tell your family's inside story. Photocopy these pages before you write on them. You will probably change your answers several times as you uncover more information.

Let me tell you about my family . . .

When I grow up, I want to be like   because

I have a lot in common with   . We both like

I am not at all like   because

We have some special/famous people in our family, such as   , who is special/famous because

The family member who tells the best jokes is

The funniest story that anyone told me was

My family gets together to celebrate   . To celebrate we

Our favorite family meal is

We went on our best family trip (when?)   . We went to

The most surprising thing I learned about my family was that

I'd still like to find out about

Tell the World

You've put your detective skills to good use and you've uncovered a lot of great facts about your family. Now's your chance to share what you've learned with the rest of the world.

Pulling It Together

Some people like to start pulling together their family history as soon as they begin digging. Others wait until they have enough material to cause an avalanche. It's up to you whether you begin putting your material together right away and then add to your family history as you go along, or whether you'd prefer to save everything up and then tackle the project all at once, perhaps during the summer.

It's Showtime!

There are so many amazing things you can do with the information you gather about your family.

You will be able to come up with a thousand and one great ideas of your own, but here are some tips to get you started:

■ THE WRITE STUFF

- Create your own family newsletter that you can e-mail to all of your relatives in far-flung places. Invite your relatives to add to it, and you'll have an incredible growing newsletter! For those who don't have e-mail access, you can print off a hard copy for them and send it out by regular mail.

- Write and illustrate a funny family book with the funniest stories you have collected about the members of your family. (You may want to check with everyone first before you publish the tales, just so nobody's feelings get hurt.) Don't forget to add in one or two stories about yourself! It will be a great pass-around for family parties.

- Ask each of your relatives to share a favorite recipe and then put them all together in a family cookbook. You could do it on the computer, or ask everyone to send in a handwritten recipe and then photocopy the pages and staple them together in a book. Be sure to give each recipe a fun name, such as "Uncle Al's Awesome Applesauce" or "Grandma Smith's Incredible Disappearing Gingerbread." It's a delicious way to celebrate what's special about your family.

■ IN THE SPOTLIGHT

- Write a play or a puppet show based on some of the funny or interesting stories that relatives have told you. Nab your brothers, sisters, or cousins and talk them into performing it with you at the next family get-together. You can borrow some clothing and some music from the right time period to help set the mood (see page 26).

- If you have been recording interviews with family members on audiotape or videotape, you can play a few minutes of edited highlights of your interviews at an upcoming family gathering. Ten to 15 minutes is usually the longest people will want to listen or watch. Five great minutes is ideal. Time it!

- Start a club and encourage your friends to do some family detective work of their own so you can swap tales and have a school or neighborhood display.

- Ask your teacher if you can bring in your family history project—and maybe even your grandma or grandpa!—for show-and-tell.

Mother mallards can keep close watch over their ducklings because the position of their eyes allows them to see what's behind them without turning their necks. (And you thought your parents had eyes in the backs of their heads!)

- Label a large sheet of paper "Family Hands." At a family get-together, have as many relatives as possible make, and autograph, their handprint. Ask them to either trace the shape of their hand using bright-colored washable markers, or dip their hand in washable paint and press it against the paper. If you can't do it in person, ask your relatives to send you photocopies of their hands, which you can trace in color. Then hang "Family Hands" on the wall.

■ ART ATTACK

- Make a huge family tree chart that covers a whole wall of your room! It will show how all of the various branches of your family fit together. You can buy a ready-made chart or make your own. Check out the sample on page 12.

- Collect lots of family memorabilia, such as old photographs, toys, swatches of fabric, postcards, and ticket stubs. Make color photocopies of everything and then use the color photocopies to create a scrapbook about your family, or make a collage for your wall.

Final Words

Don't hang up your detective hat too soon. Your detective work is never really finished. Just when you think you're done, you'll stumble across another long-lost relative or someone in your family will have another baby. Genealogy is a hobby that can last forever. That's what makes it so much fun. Happy digging!

Ancestor	Anyone from whom you are directly descended. Your parents, grandparents, or great-grandparents, and so on.
Descendants	The children, grandchildren, and so on of a particular person.
Family tree	A chart that shows how people are related to each other in a family.
Gene	A unit of heredity that is passed from a parent to a child.
Genealogy	The study of the history of a family.
Generation	All the people born at a particular time.
Given name(s)	The names that your parents gave you—usually your first and middle names.
Heredity	The passing-on of physical or mental characteristics from ancestor to descendants.
In-law	Someone who is related to you by marriage. Your sister's husband would be your brother-in-law.
Maiden name	A woman's name prior to marriage. Some women keep their maiden names after marriage, while others take their husband's family name instead.
Maternal ancestor	An ancestor on your mother's side of the family.
Memorabilia	Items that have sentimental value to the members of a family (old photographs, letters, cards, and so on).
Paternal ancestor	An ancestor on your father's side of the family.
Relative	A person who belongs to the same family as another.
Siblings	Brothers and sisters.
Surname	The name members of a family share (also called a last name or a family name).
Trait	An inherited characteristic.